¡Hola Madrid!
A Kid's Guide To Madrid, Spain

Photography By John D. Weigand
Poetry By Penelope Dyan

Bellissima Publishing, LLC
Jamul, California
www.bellissimapublishing.com

copyright © 2012 by Penny D. Weigand & John D. Weigand

All rights reserved. No part of this book may be
reproduced or transmitted in any form or by any means,
electronic or mechanical, including photocopying,
recording, or by any other means, or by any information or
storage retrieval system, without permission from the publisher.

ISBN 978-1-61477-031-2
First Edition

"I do not seek, I find."

PABLO PICASSO

1881-1973

¡ Hola Madrid!
Bellissima Publishing, LLC

Introduction

Madrid, Spain is more than a stopover place on your way to somewhere else in Europe. It is a place where your eyes can soak up sites that have history. In America, everything is very new in comparison to what you will see in Europe; and by getting out and seeing a place far away, even if it is in a book like this one, you can absorb and feel the heart of the place. Madrid, has a splendid mixture of architecture and art that makes a feast for the eyes. (This is not to say you should not also have a feast for your tummy.) Find out what you can eat in Spain that even Spanish kids eat, kids just like you. A book can't tell you everything about a city; however, this award winning author, California lawyer and former teacher, Penelope Dyan, and John D. Weigand are doing their best to show you things a kid might like to see and do when they go to Madrid, Spain. This book is a beginning point on your way to learning all about Madrid, not an ending point. There is a free video you can also watch on YouTube (by Penelope Dyan and John D. Weigand) where you can see even more! Use this book as a part of your very own learning tool collection, and then use the tools in your toolbox to build your knowledge of all things!

¡ Hola Madrid!
Bellissima Publishing, LLC

¡Hola Madrid!
A Kid's Guide To Madrid, Spain

Photography By John D. Weigand
Poetry By Penelope Dyan

Whether you go up or down
may reveal whether you are
going TO or FROM
Madrid's central downtown.
You can take the subway,
a car or a bus,
because getting around Madrid
is really NO fuss.

There are Spanish arches!
You peek and walk through!
(Where you go in Madrid
is all up to you.)
There is one thing you will find.
That is, that as to being a city,
Madrid is ONE of a kind.
But all cities are originals,
and this you well know.
And it is NOT because
I told you so!

Fountains bubble, drip, swish,
plop splash and spout.
This is (some of) what Madrid
is all about.
But please do NOT go into
fountains simply to play,
especially on a cold,
blustery day.
To do that would be very bad,
and make your mother
oh so sad.

Here is something you need to learn: "Rice that is not stirred will most certainly burn."*
The Edificio Metrópolis. started in in 1907, wasn't finished until 1911!.
So you see they really stirred THIS pot.
Through the years building it, they stirred it a lot!

* Arroz que no se menea, se quema.

Madrid, Spain
has its share of things sweet,
but apples, and carrots are a
healthier treat.
(You could go and ask a horse,
but he WOULD probably prefer
oats AND molasses, of course!)

In the middle of the Plaza de la Independencia stands the Alcala Gate. It took nine years to build and was finished in 1778!*

* In 1764 King Carlos III commissioned the Italian architect Sabatini to construct a large gate to replace a small 16th century baroque gate, built by King Philips III. Carlos III felt the gate, which marked the eastern boundary of the city, was too small for the important gateway to Aragon. It is now a national monument, and in the 19th century the Puerta de Alcalá was moved to its current location at the Plaza de la Independencia.

In the Prado Museum* you see paintings of many kinds. The "second" Mona Lisa* was one of its finds! You never know, when you start, where and when you will find a true work of art.

*The Prado Museum was hosting 180 works of art from the Russian State Hermitage Museum at the time this photo was taken.

* A copy of the Mona Lisa has been discovered in the Prado that was painted in Leonardo Davinci's studio and was created side by side with the original that hangs in the Louvre.

Men in capes and top hats,
grace the Plaza Mayor square,
You wonder why
they are standing there.
(They look ready, after all,
for a state affair or a ball.)
Brick buildings and arches
lead to the street.
Your tummy grumbles.
You want to eat!

The dome of this church
stands out against the blue
and the clouds of the sky.
The church steeple looks down
from quite near by.
Suddenly from the steeple,
the church bells ring.
For a moment you think
you hear angels sing.

Then right before your eyes
(you see, of course)
two policemen
wearing blue and yellow---
each riding on a HORSE!

The Spaniards say,
"Hunger sharpens the wit."
You want to stop to rest a bit.
(You laugh because
you see this sign.)
Perritos calientes (hot dogs)
are a VERY good find!
You stop to eat
a perrito caliente or two,
like ANY kid in Spain would do!

Sadly from Madrid
you will soon be gone.
Dad promises you'll return
before too long.
You put a brand new smile
on your face,
Because you REALLY do
like THIS place!

De ilusión también se vive.

"A Life is not only about 'getting there' but also about "dreaming of getting there."

A Spanish Proverb

www.ingramcontent.com/pod-product-compliance
Ingram Content Group UK Ltd.
Pitfield, Milton Keynes, MK11 3LW, UK
UKHW060136240426
12048UKWH00002B/57